Southwest Writers Series 31

General Editor: James W. Lee

Wayne Gard

Historian of the West

BY RAMON F. ADAMS

52804

STECK-VAUGHN COMPANY   AUSTIN, TEXAS
An Intext Publisher

Born and educated in Texas, Ramon F. Adams received his M.A. degree at Austin College, class of 1912. He has published sixteen books, written introductions for eight others, chapters for twelve, and edited two others as well as writing numerous magazine articles. He is a former member of the Texas State Historical Association, the West Texas Historical Society, the Panhandle-Plains Historical Society, the Dallas Press Club, the New York, Los Angeles, Chicago, Kansas City and Denver Westerners. He is at present a member of the Western History Association, the Texas Institute of Letters, the Southwest Writers, the English Westerners Society of London. He was awarded a Meritorious Service Award by Austin College in 1962, and an honorary degree of Doctor of Literature by this same institution in 1968. His lifetime hobby has been collecting the language of the cattle country and books on the West.

ISBN 0-8114-3894-5
Library of Congress Catalog Card Number 73-123044
Copyright © 1970 by Steck-Vaughn Company, Austin, Texas
All Rights Reserved. Printed and Bound in the United States of America

Wayne Gard

Historian of the West

Wayne Gard
Historian of the West

EVERY READER AND COLLECTOR of Western Americana is acquainted with the books and magazine articles of Wayne Gard and knows him to be an accurate and meticulous historian. Through his careful research and sound scholarship, he has brought to light phases of the history of the American West neglected by other historians. He has helped rescue from distorted Hollywood images, and to show in their true light, such frontier figures as the cowboy, the buffalo hunter, the gunman, the vigilante, and the peace officer.

Gard, the son of Guy William Gard and Winnie Iona (Sanford) Gard, was born in the small town of Brocton, Edgar County, Illinois, on June 21, 1899. Though his full name is Sanford Wayne Gard, he never uses the Sanford except for documents that require his full name.

His ancestors came to America from England and Germany before the American Revolution. In time, from their various homes in the states of New York, New Jersey, and Pennsylvania, later generations migrated westward into Ohio, Indiana, Illinois, and Kansas. Most of them took up farming.

Both of his parents were born and reared in Cumberland County, Illinois, near the village of Hazel Dell. When Wayne was born, his father was clerking in a grocery store; but Guy William Gard was ambitious, and though progress came slowly with many setbacks, he finally became the head of a corporation that had stores in nine cities in northern Illinois.

The family moved from Brocton back to the smaller community of Hazel Dell when Wayne was a year old. There his father worked in the store of his ailing father-in-law, and shortly afterward, with a partner, began operating a larger general country store and a nearby poultry house.

1

As in most small towns, life in Hazel Dell was simple. Playing games, wading in the creek, fishing for crawdads, trapping for rabbits, and going to a one-room school occupied the boys' time.

In 1908, when Wayne was eight and a half years of age, the family moved to the drier climate of Iola, Kansas, because of his mother's ill health. Scarcely more than a year later, they moved to the little town of Le Hunt, near Independence. Then in January, 1910, when the father became a traveling salesman for a flour mill, they moved to Chillicothe, Missouri.

Here Wayne became interested in the West. In those days the Buffalo Bill-Pawnee Bill Wild West show had a great influence on young boys of the neighborhood. After seeing this show, the boys often organized a Wild West show of their own, riding wild stick horses and even painting their faces with the juice from the hulls of black walnuts to make themselves look more like Indians. For this trick they usually received a reprimand when they got home, since it took weeks for the stain to wear off.

While living in Chillicothe, Wayne began to read more books. By now he had abandoned the Horatio Alger novels for more serious books on history and travel, which were borrowed from the school library.

Early in 1912 a change in the sales territory brought another move of the family to Jacksonville, Illinois. In the late summer of 1913, just before time to enter high school, Wayne took a job delivering the evening newspaper, the *Courier*, thus beginning an association with journalism and printer's ink which was to last for more than half a century.

In the fall of 1917 Wayne entered Illinois College in Jacksonville. He lived at home, but had to work at various jobs to help pay his expenses. In the summer after his freshman year, he worked at a steel assembly plant, and after his junior year became a newspaper reporter. He majored in English and joined the Phi Alpha Literary Society. On October 1, 1918, he volunteered in the United States Army, but since the Armistice came only six weeks later, his was a short military service.

During his college years Wayne became interested in writing. In his senior year he was associate and literary editor of the student magazine, the *Rambler*, and editor of the college yearbook, the *Rig Veda*. Also in his senior year and for four years thereafter, he wrote light lyric poems that were published in the *Chicago Tribune*, the *New York Herald*, several magazines including the *Poetry Review* (London), and a number of anthologies. His most popular poem, "Hollyhocks," was reprinted in *Braithwaithe's Anthology of Magazine Verse* and the poetry page of *Literary Digest* and later was set to music by the noted composer Carrie Jacobs Bond.

Because he had read so many travel books when younger and had not gotten to see foreign service in World War I, he applied for a foreign job after graduation, and he secured the position of teaching English and history in a high school in Rangoon, Burma, then still a province of British India. Preceding his trip to Burma, he had worked most of the summer on Jacksonville's morning paper, the *Daily Journal*. He sailed from New York in August, 1921, and the trip gave him eleven days in England and two in Egypt before he reached the port of Rangoon.

In Rangoon Gard learned much about the Orient through his Buddhist, Hindu, and Moslem students. He also traveled to other Burmese cities, such as Moulmein, Mandalay, Maymyo, and Bhamo, and at one time rode horseback into the wild Chinese mountain province of Yunnan, noted for opium and bandits.

He lived for nearly three years in Burma, and in addition to his teaching, he served as a part-time correspondent for the Associated Press of New York. In this capacity, he reported a visit of the Prince of Wales, and one by Sir Rabindranath Tagore, the Hindu poet, playwright, and philosopher who had won the Nobel Prize for literature in 1913. Gard was on the committee which welcomed and entertained Tagore. He also interviewed for the AP the long-deposed queen of Burma, Supayalat, who was mentioned in Rudyard Kipling's poem "Mandalay."

As a correspondent for the Associated Press, Gard was highly complimented by the superintendent of foreign service. While in Rangoon, he also wrote a few magazine articles. One, a short piece on the Burmese nationalist movement, was published in January, 1923, by *The Nation*.

Before he left Rangoon in the spring of 1924, Gard decided that, instead of continuing with teaching, he wanted to make writing his life's work. He was granted the one journalism fellowship offered each year by the Medill School of Journalism of Northwestern University. Upon his return to America, he was offered a summer job in New York by the Associated Press, but turned it down to go to work on the two newspapers of Jacksonville, Illinois, which were under the same ownership. In addition to reporting and editing news that summer, he edited an experimental Sunday book page in the *Journal*.

As a graduate student at Northwestern, he served on the editorial staff of the *Daily Northwestern* and as an assistant on the journalism faculty. Frequently he contributed book reviews to the Friday book section of the *Chicago Evening Post*, then edited by Llewellyn Jones.

Obtaining his master's degree in 1925, he began work as a wire editor in the Chicago office of the Associated Press. In spite of his earlier decision against teaching, he quit in September to accept a post teaching journalism at Grinnell College in Grinnell, Iowa. Just before reporting to the college he went to Dubuque, Iowa, where on September 10 he married Hazel Anna Dell, whom he had known in his college days and to whom he had become engaged by correspondence while he was in Burma.

During his five years at Grinnell he spent most of the summers in newspaper work. In this period he also wrote articles for such magazines as *The Independent, Plain Talk, The Christian Century,* and *The International Book Review,* as well as reviews for the book page of the *Chicago Daily News*. He also edited a small magazine, the *Tanager*. In 1926 he was on the Chicago staff of the Associated Press and in 1929 on that of the *Chicago Daily News*. In 1926 he also wrote, on contract, a concise volume entitled *Book Reviewing* for a series of journalism handbooks being published in New York by Alfred A. Knopf. Released in 1927, this book, the first in its field, was favorably reviewed and was used in many universities.

On April 22 of this same year a son, Christopher, was born to the Gards. With this addition to the family, Wayne became more ambitious to increase his education, and in the summer of 1928 he entered Columbia University, New York, to continue his study of history. In 1930 he became editorial writer for the *Des Moines Register* and *Tribune*, and at the same time continued his magazine writing, contributing articles to *Current History, The Nation, The New Republic, North American Review,* and two of the Conde Nast publications, *House and Garden* and *Vanity Fair.* Four of these articles were reprinted in *Reader's Digest.* After his first year in Des Moines, he also became a part-time teacher of journalism at Drake University.

Soon after this, in 1932, Gard accepted a temporary job as an assistant editor of *Vanity Fair* in New York. While there, he contributed frequent articles to the magazine in addition to editing the work of other contributors. He returned in the fall of that year to Des Moines to continue his part-time teaching at Drake and do free-lance writing. There he also handled public relations for an adult education forum of the public school system.

Gard went to Dallas, Texas, in August, 1933, to join the staff of the *Dallas Morning News* at the invitation of G. B. Dealey, its publisher and the dean of Texas newspapermen. Here he remained for thirty-one years, until he retired. After a few weeks on the copy desk to get acquainted with the newspaper's style and brief periods in writing city and state news, he became one of the paper's editorial writers. Not only did he write editorials, but he also contributed signed articles and many book reviews for the Sunday book page. Several of his editorials won state and national awards.

Soon after Gard became acclimated to Texas, he developed a strong interest in its history—and in fact the history of the whole Southwest and West. This interest was reflected in his writings for the *News* and also in the articles he wrote for various magazines. During his first years in Texas, his magazine articles— chiefly for *Current History, American Mercury, New Republic, Nation's Business,* and *Christian Century*—dealt largely with current political and economic problems. It was not long before his interest shifted to historical subjects, and he started writing for a different group of magazines, such as *American Heritage, Ameri-*

can *West, Cattleman, Western Horseman, Southwestern Histori-cal Quarterly,* and *Southwest Review.*

Gard and his wife took an active interest in the social and cultural life of Dallas and frequently attended symphony concerts and the opera, as well as concerts by other visiting musical artists. He had joined the professional journalism fraternity, Sigma Delta Chi, in his first year at Grinnell and became a charter member of the Dallas professional chapter in 1935, when the national convention of the organization was held in Dallas. He became its second president in 1936; and in 1940 he headed the national awards committee, and as a member of the national executive council, attended the national convention in Des Moines.

The *News* sent Gard on a number of trips through Texas, and these gave him the opportunity to become acquainted with the state and its history. In 1934 he made a week's swing about Texas to write a series of articles on roadside developments, and he repeated this process in 1936. On occasion he made trips on his own initiative, such as visiting the King Ranch in 1936, and he toured some of the state parks, including the Big Bend area in 1940. Ten years later he attended the annual reunion of old XIT Ranch cowhands at Dalhart, and such visits stirred his interest in the history of the cattle country.

On occasion the *News* sent him on trips outside the state, such as one to Chicago to observe and report the Republican National Convention. But the thing which created a deeper interest in Texas and Western history was his ten months of working to prepare a historical issue of the News that was published October 1, 1935. This interest was spurred also by his writing for the *Baltimore Evening Sun.* During the years he was on the *News's* staff, he served as Texas editorial correspondent of the Baltimore paper, contributing frequent articles to its editorial page.

In the spring of 1935 Gard was asked by the editor of the *Evening Sun* to contribute a piece on the Texas Rangers. This subject was timely since, after the Ranger force had deteriorated while being used for political patronage by the Fergusons, Governor James V. Allred had asked the Texas Legislature to reorganize and rejuvenate this organization and restore it to its former usefulness. Since he did not know much of this organization's background, Gard immediately started buying books and doing other research, some of which was from stories he found in the *Galveston News* file in the *Dallas Morning News* library.

From his research on the Rangers he became deeply interested in the career of Sam Bass, especially his pursuit and death. During 1935 and early 1936 many Texas writers were writing historical books to coincide with the Texas Centennial, scheduled for the latter year. Gard decided to join them by writing the first really dependable biography of this popular outlaw. He immediately wrote letters to Indiana, where Bass had grown up, seeking information about his boyhood and ancestry, about which earlier accounts had said little. In fact, this book is the only one which goes into Bass's ancestry.

His inquiries to Indiana produced two series of certified documents, one on the adoption of the Bass children by an uncle and the other on the administration of their father's estate by another uncle. The latter included a record of the sale of 124 household items and farm implements on hand at the father's death.

Gard also persuaded his youngest brother, Louis, a young lawyer in Illinois, to go to Indiana and talk with the surviving relatives of the outlaw. Louis talked with two of Sam's brothers, a cousin, and an old aunt, and he saw the family Bible and other records. This helped greatly in filling out the fragmentary information on Sam's boyhood. Seeking information on Bass's Texas experiences, Gard went to Denton County to visit the Bass hideouts and to talk with several persons who had known him. These included Charley Brim, who wrote some of the Bass letters; Charley Tucker, who as a jockey rode Bass's Denton Mare; and Will Williams, a Denton historian who gave valuable help.

Seeking further information, Gard went to Fort Worth, Texas, where he talked with Jake Zurn, who had been station agent at Mesquite at the time of the last train robbery of the Bass gang. He followed the Bass trail to Round Rock, examined the bullet holes from the street battle, and heard the story of the fight from a woman who had witnessed the battle. He spent most of a summer vacation in a hot and poorly lighted attic at The University of Texas, obtaining information from the 1876 files of the *Dallas Times Herald* and other newspapers. He also had the good fortune to talk with Ranger June Peak, who had chased Bass all over Denton County, and had the loan of a manuscript on Bass done by the late B. C. Jefferson, editorial writer of the *Dallas Times Herald.*

In his biography of Sam Bass, Gard stuck to a policy of strict realism. He neither exaggerated Bass as a bloodthirsty outlaw with notches on his gun, nor showed any maudlin sentimentality toward him. He was not misled by the stories of robbing the rich to help the poor—such tales as had often been applied to Robin Hood and Jesse James. Instead, he viewed Bass as a real person, an orphan boy who was misled by horse-race gambling into robbing stagecoaches and trains.

So from talking with people who had known Bass, from court records, from early newspaper accounts, and from the published accounts by contemporaries of Bass, Gard learned all he could about the bandit, then traced in detail the trail of his life against a frontier background.

In the fall of 1935, when his manuscript was only half finished, Houghton Mifflin Company of Boston heard of Gard's project through John McGinnis, Professor of English at Southern Methodist University and editor of the book page of the *Dallas Morning News;* and they asked to see the manuscript. The completed manuscript was sent to them early in January, 1936, and it was published in late July, about six weeks after the opening of the Texas Centennial.

Although interested in folk tales, Gard never forgets that he is first of all a historian. In *Sam Bass* he recounts some of the stories about this celebrated bandit, but is careful to relegate them to his final chapter, "Texas Robin Hood." Bass perhaps received this title from the fact that he spent his share of the gold pieces from the Union Pacific robbery freely. The fable about his burying money throughout the territory is merely folklore. Because he received less than $2000, which from all four of his Texas train robberies was divided equally among his gang of from four to six confederates, there was very little money left for him to bury; and he had spent his last twenty dollar gold piece on his way to Round Rock.

When one gives it some thought, it is strange how Bass became such a noted character, for he was no gunman, no killer, and a very sorry holdup man. Perhaps the song written about him and sung by so many cowboys was responsible for some of his popularity.

"Many of the legends that took root in cattle camps and hearthsides magnified Sam's crimes as well as the size of his loot," writes Gard. "Most of these stories were as fictitious as that of the Texas verse writer who described Bass as stealing a pig when the Indiana youth was only ten years old. . . . Although sheriffs and Rangers seldom sighted him, legendary encounters with the elusive Sam were reported from many places" (Sam Bass, pp. 241-42).

After telling of various parties digging for Sam's gold after they had bought "an old penciled map that showed where Sam had buried two hundred thousand dollars' worth of gold bullion and other valuables" (p. 247), Gard closes his book with "Where the searchers will strike next, no one can tell. As long as the Sam Bass legends persist, no Texan can be sure that he will not wake some morning to find a ton of earth removed from his front yard by some romanticist who has just come into possession of the one authentic map" (p. 247). Gard refuses to get himself out on a limb by saying that a pistol or a hat claimed to have belonged to Bass was really his or to authenticate any of the legends about digging for gold that Sam was said to have buried.

This first Western book by Gard received many very favorable reviews from such expert critics as Walter Prescott Webb, Stanley Walker, and Joseph Henry Jackson. Walter Prescott Webb wrote in his review of this book in the Dallas Morning News:

. . . Wayne Gard has done a biography that bears the stamp of authenticity in every sentence. We can be thankful that the author has put no imaginary words into Sam Bass's mouth, has not psychoanalyzed him, or tried to crawl inside Sam's mind to tell us how Sam looked at the world or why he had a grievance against it. . . . The whole story of Bass is told here for the first time, told so accurately, so dispassionately, and with such wealth of detail—names, dates, and specific events—that the job of telling the truth about Sam Bass is now completed. . . . The fashion is to romanticize about Western bad men and about Western subjects in general, but this author has stuck to ascertainable facts with commendable reserve, and told a better story than the romancers (July 26, 1936).

In his Foreword Gard writes:

To winnow fact from legend in the story of Sam Bass has not been easy, especially since most of the people who knew him have died and courthouse fires have destroyed many records that might have thrown light on his exploits. Unlike some desperadoes who lived to old age and wrote autobiographies, Bass died illiterate as well as young. Despite the efforts resulting in this book, there are still gaps in his story. To fill these gaps with fictional details is a strong temptation, but in this instance the temptation has been resisted (p. iv).

For many years biographers of Sam Bass and other writers have had Jim Murphy committing suicide, but again Gard "tells it like it was" when he writes in a late chapter:

To his [Murphy's] fear of sudden death from avengers of Sam Bass, an eye ailment soon added to his woes. On the morning of June 7, 1879, less than a year after the street battle at Round Rock, Jim went to Lipscomb's drugstore on the west side of the square and asked Dr. Ed McMath, a young physician who had his office there, to treat his eyes. Somehow a quantity of the atropine the doctor gave him for his eyes got into his throat. Murphy soon became ill, and most of the day he lay in the drugstore. Between spells of convulsions, he would light his pipe and plead, "Can't you do something for me, Ed?" The doctor did what he could; but in the afternoon Jim was taken home, and that evening the "spy hero" passed to a reward perhaps more generous than the one given him in song and legend (p. 235).

Thus is corrected that fable of Murphy's committing suicide from the fear that Jackson was out to kill him.

Bibliographers, writers, and researchers check Gard's book with confidence for correct dates and correct information, for it is accurate and dependable in every detail. This book, long out-of-print, brings a high price when one is fortunate enough to locate a copy; but in 1969 the University of Nebraska Press brought it out in a paperback edition, with the original halftone illustrations, in its popular series of Bison Books.

With the publication of *Sam Bass* came the election of Gard to membership in the recently-formed Texas Institute of Letters, a select organization which is still steadily growing in importance for those interested in writing. Gard also joined the Texas Folklore Society and has appeared on several annual programs of both these organizations. His strongest interest, however, is in the state's oldest learned society, the Texas State Historical Association, of which he is a life member. Elected a fellow in 1954, he served as vice-president and later as president from 1968 to 1969. He has been faithful in attending the annual meetings in Austin and has been chosen as speaker at its luncheons and dinners.

After the publication of *Sam Bass*, Gard did not start work on another book for a time because his newspaper work was exacting and for several years he was teaching a downtown evening course in magazine writing for Southern Methodist University.

In 1946 the *Dallas Morning News* established a five-day week, and this gave Gard additional leisure time. He had already begun collecting material for a book to trace the development of law and order in the early West. This he entitled *Frontier Justice*. He was helped in this endeavor by a modest grant from the Texas State Historical Association, which had for this purpose a fund from the Rockefeller Foundation.

In his Foreword to *Frontier Justice* the author writes:

Gathering material for this work has taken the author over many western trails, including that of the invading cattlemen in Wyoming. He has gone also to the weatherbeaten shack of Roy Bean in the western plains of Texas, to the reports of dauntless Ranger captains in Austin, and to the records of Judge Isaac C. Parker's court in Fort Smith. While primary sources of information have been used as far as practicable, a book covering so wide a territory, so long a period, and so diverse a field could hardly be written without the author's relying heavily on the spade work of other searchers and writers in individual fields (p. vi).

Gard also spent two weeks in Austin doing research in the Texas Archives and the University of Texas Library. On vacation in 1947, he and his brother Paul went to Colorado and Wyoming and in the latter state followed the route of the Johnson County invasion of 1892, visiting the battle sites and seeing the bullet holes made by the attackers at the T A Ranch.

In *Frontier Justice* Gard writes the following:

Civilization took a rapid stride across the American West. In the short span of two generations settlers witnessed a rise from savagery to social stability that in some parts of the world took several thousand years. To some of the participants the taming of the West seemed slow. Certainly it was marked by violence—almost every community had its blazing guns and dangling ropes. Yet, as history goes, the transition from the bloody tomahawk of the painted savage to the polished gavel of the black-robed judge came with bounding speed (p. v).

The book shows that the six-shooter and the hanging rope, like the plow and riata, had a part in the taming of the early West.

During the writing of this book, Gard was signally honored by his alma mater, Illinois College, in his selection as an alumnus member of Phi Beta Kappa, the national honorary society founded in 1776. Since the Illinois College chapter was not chartered until 1932, he had no opportunity to be elected as a student. Later he served a year as president of the Dallas Association of Phi Beta Kappa.

His *Frontier Justice* was published by the University of Oklahoma Press in 1949 and was immediately and enthusiastically received by readers and reviewers. In his Introduction Gard wrote: "This book is an informal study of the rise of order and law west of the Mississippi, where order often came before law" (p. vi). The book covers the period from 1836 to the close of the century. He starts out with the Indian troubles, emphasizing the Indian's cruelty in battle and the white man's retaliation.

There is a chapter on the bloody feud of East Texas known as the Regulator and Moderator War, perhaps the first of the many feuds to be the scourge of Texas. This feud held back the young Republic; people were afraid to settle there, and the land became practically worthless. The author deals with other Texas feuds, such as the Taylor-Sutton feud (the longest and bloodiest of them all), the Horrell-Higgins feud, and the Mason County War. Even the Lincoln County War of New Mexico and the Pleasant Valley War of Arizona are dealt with in some detail.

This is indeed a book of conflict for law and order. The author covers thoroughly the many struggles of the raw West with its feuds, sheep and range wars, relations between early settlers and Indians, vigilante activities, and the work of the Western marshals and sheriffs and the Texas Rangers. It reveals the clashing economic interests of rival groups of stockmen that led to battles for grass and water. In addition to strife between sheepmen and cattlemen, there were range wars between cattle kings who wanted fenced ranches and small cowmen who were determined to keep the open range with its free grass.

Of the prairies and in the mining camps, Gard has the following to say:

> Orthodox law enforcement often lagged behind the need to punish troublesome offenders. Where officials were helpless and jails were far away, citizens had to work together as vigilantes. They made their own laws on the spot, caught horsethieves and other outlaws, and hanged them to the nearest cottonwood. Sometimes they imposed overly severe penalties or executed the wrong men; but usually they were fair, and their activities discouraged crime. The work of the vigilance committees was a form of social action and a step toward the setting up of statutory courts (p. v).

The book's greatest contribution to frontier history is no doubt the section on range wars, in which the author gives a good account of the Johnson County War of Wyoming and the war between sheepmen and cattlemen for the range. He also gives some new information on the Texas fence-cutters' conflict in 1883.

In the West's struggle for law, the author does not neglect the vigilantes of California or Montana's later efforts to rid itself of outlaws and road agents. Neither does he neglect the Texas Rangers, the sheriffs, and the marshals in depicting the bloody and primitive law enforcements in the West's struggle to rise from savagery to civilization. The period with which he deals is the West's most interesting and thrilling era of evolution.

During the writing of *Frontier Justice*, Gard read a chapter from the manuscript as a paper on the fence-cutters at the 1947 meeting of the Texas State Historical Association in Austin. This paper was published in the *Southwestern Historical Quarterly*, LI, (July, 1947), and later reprinted as a separate pamphlet under the title of *The Fence-Cutters*. It is now a scarce collector's item.

Often quoted is Gard's description of the drouth that contributed to the fence troubles:

> Drouth hit the Texas cow country a staggering blow in the summer of 1883. The sky was empty except for the blazing sun that parched and cracked the earth. Dust hovered over the plains and settled on what was left of the brown, shrunken grass. From the coals of careless campers or the sparks of locomotives, fires raced over many of the pastures, leaving only charred, blackened turf. When even the stubble was gone, the cattle browsed on chaparrals, munched prickly pear, and chewed the blooms of Spanish dagger.
>
> Still worse than the lack of enough grass was the scarcity of water. Creeks that had served vast herds were so dry that a crawfish could not wet his whiskers. Settlers on the upper reaches of the Brazos and the Colorado said they never had seen those rivers so low. In some streams the trickle which still flowed was so salty that cattle refused to drink it. Water holes which had lasted through other hot summers dried up. Some cattle that waded into the mud to suck up the ooze and green scum sank into the mire and suffocated.
>
> Leathery longhorns, toughened to hardship and scant fare, were crazed by thirst. They rolled their tongues in agony and bawled for water. Day by day their moaning grew weaker. Their bodies thinned, and their eyes became more sunken. From some of the herds many head were lost, first the cows with young calves, then the calves and yearling steers. The smaller cattlemen suffered first and most severely. Those who could move their piteously lowing herds to better pasture

and water did so but found their stock restless and hard to control (pp. 104-05).

Among the many favorable reviews of this book is one by Stanley Walker in the New York Herald Tribune. "Mr. Gard's service," he writes, "has been to winnow out certain inaccuracies and windy improbabilities, to boil down this sprawling material into concise form, and to present it all as one coherent story" (New York Herald Tribune, September 25, 1949).

Clarence S. Paine, in Nebraska History, wrote:

There have been many collections of the lives and deaths of the badmen of the frontier, but this reviewer has never before come across an anthology of the forces for law and order. This book is just that. Moreover, it has a welcome new approach. With objectivity rather than the sensationalism all too common to books on Indian fighting, outlaws, and peace officers, the author has succeeded in producing a book at once scholarly yet dramatic. . . . Mr. Gard has drawn from most if not all of the recognized published secondary sources, and in addition has added a good deal of documentation from original records published and unpublished. The index is a veritable Who's Who of outlaws and law enforcement officers. The book is a distinct contribution to Western Americana (XXXI, March, 1950).

Gard describes with thoroughness life in the raw on the Western frontier between the year 1836 and the close of the century, telling of brave women and the part they played in making a wild country a civilized place in which to live; of determined men and the vital roles they played in making their own laws, primitive, perhaps, but effective. He covers the entire West and tells of the feuds, wars, and lawlessness of every state as he goes. That the book is well annotated shows that the author had delved deeply into the available published records.

Later this book, among others, was chosen by a committee of distinguished scholars, headed by the librarian of Yale University, for inclusion in the permanent White House Library.

Gard was soon casting about for a subject for another book. He had written many articles on oil problems for the Dallas Morning

News, the *Baltimore Evening Sun*, *New Republic*, and *American Mercury*. This field had held his interest for some time. He knew, for example, that there was a great dramatic story to be done about the wildcatter "Dad" Joiner and his discovery of the East Texas field. But after giving the subject serious thought, he found that transportation would be difficult during the limited time he could be free for research.

Later, however, he wrote a pamphlet entitled *The First 100 Years of Texas Oil and Gas*, published in Dallas by the Texas Mid-Continent Oil and Gas Association in 1966. The pamphlet is divided into decades from 1866 to 1965 and tells the history of Texas oil from the Reconstruction days after the Civil War to modern days when the production of oil became such a vivid force, not only to Texas but to the nation as well. This pamphlet was published in celebration of the centennial of the first producing well; and the Association issued 25,000 copies, sending copies to all Texas school libraries and to all seventh-grade history teachers in the state.

After a period of uncertainty as to which subject to write a book about, Gard finally chose the Chisholm Trail because this was more in line with his previous subjects, and his interest in the cattle industry had been steadily growing through his research. In this he made a wise choice, for *The Chisholm Trail* has become one of his best-loved books, having brought him many honors and enhanced his reputation as a historian.

For this book he found valuable manuscript material in the libraries of Austin, Texas. He also culled many details from the stories he found in newspaper files of these libraries as well as of the Fort Worth Library. Accompanied by his son, Chris, he then followed the route of the trail minutely, making the trek in the spring so that he could check on the condition of the young grass at the time the trail drive would start north.

Thus he was able to write in the book:

Usually the spring drive started when the rolling Texas prairies looked their best. The grass was making the ranges green again. Flowers added splotches of color to many of the prairies and hillsides. There were patches of bluebonnets and yellow blossoms of wild mustard, along with the white of the prickly poppy and the scarlet of the Indian paintbrush. The mesquite was putting out its lacy, waving foliage; and leaf buds on the post oaks and blackjacks were beginning to swell and burst. It was a season to make the young cowboy restless and eager to go places (*The Chisholm Trail*, p. 110).

At the end of the trail, Gard visited most of the cow towns of Kansas, examining such places as the site of the Alamo Saloon in Abilene, where Wild Bill Hickok had made his headquarters. In the library and archives of the Kansas State Historical Society at Topeka, he found a wealth of material, both on the trail and the towns at its end, as well as on the behavior of the cowboys in their clashes with the troublesome city marshals.

Starting at the beginning when cattle were first introduced into this country by the early explorers, Gard tells of the millions of cattle wandering over the open ranges of Texas and the capturing and taming of wild stock. He relates the opening of the new Northern markets and the hazards of the long drive and of high spirits, both physical and liquid, when the cowboys hit the town at the end of the trail. He tells of the origin of the popular songs of the trail, of the blocking of the trail by irate citizens because of the Texas fever, and of the cattle destroying farmers' crops. He explains the economic impact of the cattle movement, probably the greatest migration of domestic animals in history, and emphasizes the human aspects of this movement of Texas longhorns to a much-needed market for a much-needed product.

The Chisholm Trail allowed Texas to dig herself out of the poverty that followed the Civil War. It lent impetus to the development and growth of the now-large packing plants of Kansas City, Chicago, and Omaha, as well as giving incentive to the building of railroads and refrigerator cars and to the breeding of cattle in the Northwest. This trail, too, was responsible for giving the cowboy such a bad name from his actions, for it was in the trail-end towns that he met people from the North and East and became such good newspaper copy. This winding trail was the cowboy's road to high adventure, one that "held the excitement of sudden stampedes, hazardous river crossings, and brushes with

Indian marauders." To be chosen to go "up the trail" was as high an honor as the early-day cowboy could expect. It meant that he had plenty of courage and daring; that he was trustworthy and possessed of that typical loyalty of rangeland. Chances are that the owner went ahead by stage or train, having turned the herd over to his cowboys and trusted them to get the cattle through safely with a minimum loss.

The book also tells of hilarious life in the Kansas towns where the herds were sold, of the songs used to prod the steers by day and to soothe them at night. Sometimes the herds were sold to other cattlemen from Montana or Wyoming, and the Texas cowboys were hired to continue driving them north. Many times it happened that the Texas cowboys fell in love with these Northern states and stayed on for the rest of their lives.

The book describes how the wild cattle were captured and branded, how they were kept strung out on the trail, and how they were protected from the white rustlers and Indian beggars. It recounts the true story of cowboy life on the trail and thus helps to correct some of the misinformation spawned in Hollywood. Even the wagon cook and the food he served are not neglected.

In preparing to write this narrative, the author talked with surviving trail drivers, made a diligent search in several states for records and manuscripts, traveled over the route of the trail several times, and visited the Kansas towns that were its chief terminals.

It is good to find an authentic account of this noted trail and of the drives conducted over it. Its significance in American life has extended to fiction and folklore in which it played a dramatic part. But Gard has stuck to facts in this significant contribution to American history. There is romance and action enough in the history of the Chisholm Trail without resorting to fiction. The author describes the many troubles of the drover, affords minute description of the trail as it progressed northward, tells of the enterprising Joseph McCoy who opened the trail, and gives some history of Jesse Chisholm (for whom the trail was named, though he never lived to see its important use). The book has a splendid bibliography and index and is well annotated, Gard's research having been thorough as usual.

Published by the University of Oklahoma Press in the spring of 1954 and illustrated with both halftones and the drawings of that splendid Western artist Nick Eggenhofer, *The Chisholm Trail* evoked more favorable reviews and greater enthusiasm than any of Gard's earlier books. The many reviews, some written by noted writers of the West, were all favorable. In the *New York Times Book Review*, Ross Santee, himself an eminent Western writer and artist, called Gard's book "a magnificent piece of work." In a review in the book page of *Time*, Charles Poore wrote: "The best story of adventure that has come this way in a fair interval is *The Chisholm Trail*, by Wayne Gard. This is a scholarly narrative, but the material of a true saga bursts from the book's learned seams. It is better reading than a dozen of the latest, largest, lustiest historical novels of the moment. The Chisholm Trail lives in Mr. Gard's book" (April 24, 1954). Later *Time* listed *The Chisholm Trail* as one of the outstanding books of 1954.

In the *Chicago Tribune* Richard Blakesley commented: "Wayne Gard's highly readable, studiously documented history begins with Jesse Chisholm. It was a lusty, romantic and dangerous era of which Gard writes so well. His account of the famous trail has that particular and vital historical interest so intriguing to Americans who glory in their proud heritage" (May 16, 1954).

Among other praise is Joseph Henry Jackson's review in the *Dallas Morning News*:

> Within a decade the trail was a legend; people argued— and still argue, though Mr. Gard's book will settle much of that—just where the Chisholm Trail had run. It had played its part, a vital one in the making of the American West. . . .
> As has been suggested, Mr. Gard, an informed scholar, sticks to the facts; his book is the product of careful and long research; he knows his sources and has gone to them, as his admirable bibliography demonstrated. But he is also the kind of historian who never lets his material get the upper hand. He is in control every minute, and since he is the one who knows the value of an anecdote or a bit of color, a first-hand record or a letter straight out of the period, there is no smell of a dusty library, or the student lamp about this story.

19

This is the kind of thing every writer who chooses some phase of the American past as his theme sets out to give us, though so few of them do (April 25, 1954).

Eugene Hollon, in the *Daily Oklahoman*, says: "Wayne Gard's exciting narrative not only deals with the economic and physical hazards of trail driving, but it also presents an excellent picture of the principal characters associated with the cattle boom and the society in which they lived" (April 25, 1954).

The late Dan Ferguson says:

> As the trends toward dissolution of trail driving begin to emerge, the story under Gard's guidance unfolds itself. The creeping paralysis to which trail driving and open range life fell a victim stemmed from the increase of farmers, the adoption of barbed wire, and the extension of the railroads.
>
> This work so soundly researched and so solidly written may well serve as collateral reading for college students and an invaluable source book for their themes and theses (*Southwestern Historical Quarterly*, LVIII, July, 1954, p. 183).

The book starts with a memorable description—praised by Carl Sandburg—of the herds strung out on the winding trail:

> Like mighty armies the herds moved slowly northward, each with its cloud of dust. The cattle grazed as they plodded along, every step taking them farther from their Texas range. The herd's only banner was the flapping canvas of the chuck wagon, its only trumpets the bawling of the cows. Yet on and on the Longhorns marched.
>
> Even those Kansans who had seen their plains darkened with buffalo herds were bewildered. Never, it seemed, had there been such an invasion as that of the half-wild cattle pouring in by the Chisholm Trail. The ferocious-looking brutes with sharp, spreading horns overflowed the prairies and crowded the banks of rivers and creeks. From a hilltop one could look for miles without seeing any end to the herds.
>
> The Longhorns that tramped up this and other dusty trails from Texas belonged to a rough breed. They were even hardier than the wind-beaten men on horseback who kept them pointed in the right direction. For nearly four

centuries they had been adapting themselves to a new world and a new way of life. They had learned to fend for themselves and to survive without human aid (*The Chisholm Trail*, p. 3).

The excellence of this book brought Gard many honors. The governor of Oklahoma appointed him an honorary colonel on his staff; the Atchison, Topeka, and Santa Fe Railroad, whose line closely followed the route of the trail, bought a thousand copies to give some of its friends; and the Texas State Historical Association elected him one of its fellows. This book also has been cited in a large number of later books, and it has been kept in print almost continually.

In 1956 the First National Bank of Dallas, which had decorated its private dining room with bronze replicas of Texas cattle brands, asked Gard to write an illustrated booklet, *Cattle Brands of Texas*, to hand to visitors as a souvenir. This booklet, which had a revised edition in the next decade, later went out-of-print; but it continues to be in demand by Texana collectors. It is probable that Gard was asked to do this booklet through the reputation he had gained from *The Chisholm Trail*.

This history of the trail was barely off the press when the author began gathering material for two other books. The first, *Fabulous Quarter Horse: Steel Dust*, published by Duell, Sloan and Pearce in the spring of 1958, was Gard's shortest book, the story of a celebrated Texas stallion that had been owned in Dallas County a century earlier. Gard had been interested in Steel Dust ever since he had written *Sam Bass* because Bass's Denton Mare, with which he had won so many races, had had Steel Dust blood.

In 1941 J. Frank Dobie wrote Gard and suggested that he go down to Ten Mile Creek and see what he could learn about the famous horse. "You are the man to trace the true history of Steel Dust," Dobie added. Such a trip, however, had to be postponed due to the press of newspaper work. But early in 1948 a short piece Gard wrote on Steel Dust in the *Dallas Morning News* brought volunteer information from descendants of the owners of Steel Dust and the owners of rival stallions of the period.

Deeper probing brought enough material, mainly through interviews, for a long article on this stallion in that year's annual September horse issue of the *Cattleman*.

As was not the case with Gard's other books on the West, the information for *Steel Dust* had to be obtained almost entirely by word of mouth—through interviews with descendants of the owners of Steel Dust and the stallions against which he was matched in races. The author was able to find only two contemporary mentions of Steel Dust. One was in a penciled entry in a studbook kept by Jack Batchler, a farmer, horse breeder, and blacksmith who lived in southern Dallas County and later in Ellis County. In his quaint spelling, he noted in April, 1864, while the Civil War was still being fought, that he had "bred big fily to Steel Dust." The other mention was in a letter written by a son of Batchler's in 1922, describing a match between Steel Dust and another steed in 1855.

To find the people who had had stories of the racing prowess of Steel Dust handed down to them, Gard visited Lancaster and Ferris and isolated farmhouses. He even checked gravestones in a cemetery to check birth dates and thus learn how old certain people were when they were associated with the famous horse. He had to overcome many difficulties in reconciling conflicting stories and in separating history from folklore.

The book is more than the story of a horse. It is a warm narrative of frontier people. It tells of a covered-wagon journey to Texas, of grass so high it could be tied over a horse's back, of a mother who wouldn't let her son ride in a race on Sunday, and of a wife who used the juice of pokeberries and *bois d'arc* balls to dye the homespun cloth for her husband's suit.

Gard continued his research until he had gathered enough other material to make a book of sixty-four pages, also illustrated by the Western artist Nick Eggenhofer. Through this little book Gard has brought to light the true story of Texas's most famous stallion and told how he became the foundation sire of the most popular strain of quarter horses in America. The quarter horse soon became the most important horse to the rancher, especially during the roundup.

Like his other books, Gard's *Steel Dust* was well received and elicited many favorable reviews. It was kept in print for a decade, and in 1969, just after it had gone out-of-print, it was republished in its entirety with the original illustrations as the leading article in *True West*.

Ross Santee, in the *Dallas Morning News*, writes:

Out of the fog of legend the author has made Steel Dust come alive. He has done a tremendous research job, all by word of mouth. In Steel Dust's day there was no racing form or sports page, there was no written record. . . .

More than as a champion sprinter it was as a sire of quarter horses that Steel Dust carved his name. The quarter horse is the work horse at the rodeo and a work horse on the range. . . . Beside his burst of speed, he has cow sense, too. To any cowboy who has ever range branded with a horse of Steel Dust blood it's not only a privilege but a job. . . . While the book is the story of Steel Dust, his ancestors and off-spring, it is the story of people as well, substantial folk who not only were a part of the land but people who had horses in their blood. . . . This book will clarify many things for many people. My only criticism is that like the short races that are so popular in the Southwest today, the book is all too short (May 18, 1958).

Jimmie Cox, in the *Fort Worth Star-Telegram*, comments:

Separating fact from fiction concerning the mighty quarter horse Steel Dust promised to be no simple matter, but the author felt that the many questions asked about the fabled animal justified an effort. The result is this readable and be-lieveable life story of the stallion that helped establish the quarter horse as a favorite on the prairies of the Southwest (May 18, 1958).

This absorbing story of Steel Dust, his ancestors, and his off-spring is the story of the quarter horse (now the favorite of all Western horses, especially for cutting out cattle). The author goes back to colonial Virginia, where Thomas Jefferson's grand-father bred and raced short horses along the James River. From there he traces the Steel Dust line down to some of the finest mounts of today.

23

Horse racing has always been a favorite sport with cowboys, and they especially liked the quarter horse for short races. Gard writes:

After the war, quarter racing became even more popular on the frontier than it had been earlier. This was only natural in the range country, where being well mounted was as important for success—and even for survival—as being well armed. For work use in the roundups and in taking longhorn herds up the Chisholm Trail, many of the cowmen preferred mounts of Steel Dust blood. They might sell their other horses in Kansas, along with the trail cattle, but they kept the Steel Dust for their own use. And if some unwary Kansan, or even some Indian along the trail, suggested a short race, the cow hand with a Steel Dust mount always was ready (*Steel Dust*, p. 38).

Gard devotes a chapter to the Denton Mare, the race horse of Sam Bass, and says that this horse was the most talked-about mare in Texas in 1875. He tells of Bass's passion for racing after the outlaw had won a few races with this horse of Steel Dust blood. Bass and Army Egan bought this chestnut sorrel mare in 1874 from a farmer because Bass saw possibilities in her. Egan was the brother of Sheriff Dan Egan, for whom Bass worked, but the sheriff objected to his younger brother's having anything to do with a race horse and even advanced Bass the money to buy out his partner.

"He let Sam keep the mare in the Egan barn," writes Gard, "but he wasn't pleased at having his hired hand dabble in a sport that was associated with gambling and fighting. The mare, he feared, would lead Sam into bad company" (p. 41).

This proved to be true, for Bass acknowledged that horse racing was what started him on the downward road. After taking the Denton Mare to San Antonio, where he and Joel Collins, a bartender, pulled off some crooked races and fleeced the Mexicans, they raced until one wealthy turfman became suspicious of Sam and got away with $4000. Sam became disgusted after this. Gard writes:

He sold the Denton Mare in San Antonio and joined Collins in trailing a herd of longhorns to Kansas. From there they went to Deadwood, where they gambled away the cattle money and—to recoup their losses—began their short careers as robbers of stagecoaches and trains. Their banditry helped to preserve the story of the Denton Mare in legend and song. Soon after the death of Sam at Round Rock in 1878, following a gun battle with Texas Rangers and other officers, cowboys on night guard began chanting the story of his tragic life (p. 47).

As with other people and animals of the West, there were legends about Steel Dust. Gard closes this interesting little book with:

> Some of the legends from other sources, of course, proved to be so far from the truth that they are interesting only as folklore. . . . Likely other folk tales of Steel Dust will appear, and even a few more bits of his history may come to light. His former haunts still are horse country. On stormy nights some of those who live on Ten Mile Creek may think they hear his whinny—and an answering neigh from old Shiloh on Bear Creek. If the two stallions could break away from their equine Valhalla, undoubtedly they would come back some night and finish that race of 1855 and thus settle for all time the question of which was the fleeter (p. 56).

The second and more important book in Gard's plans, upon which he worked in his spare time in the 1950's, was a history of buffalo hunting in the West, *The Great Buffalo Hunt*. To a large degree, this book would be a companion volume to his *The Chisholm Trail* since both centered mainly on the Great Plains and dealt largely with the two decades that followed the Civil War. For his research on this subject he was awarded a research grant by the American Philosophical Society, founded by Benjamin Franklin in Philadelphia in 1734.

Since by this time the *Dallas Morning News* was giving employees of a certain seniority vacations of three weeks instead of two, Gard found a little more time for research. When he began gathering material for *The Great Buffalo Hunt*, he already had, from earlier books, a good background of the history of the Great Plains, which provided the principal range for the vast herd of "shaggies." Also in gathering material for this book, he made six trips of a week each: one each to Topeka, Norman, Denver, and

West Texas, and two to Austin. In the Texas Panhandle he visited the site of the battle of Adobe Walls; and although few of the old buffalo hunters had survived long enough for him to interview them, he dug up memoirs that a number of them had written but never published.

Though these huge beasts could be numbered by the millions in the West soon after the Civil War, it did not take many years for systematic slaughter to destroy them almost to the point of extinction. With the thoroughness of a true historian, Gard has left little to be said upon the subject. For years the buffalo had furnished food, clothing, shelter, and implements for the Indian, and, with the exception of a few white humanitarians, the Indian was the only one to protest this wholesale slaughter of his sustenance. But in spite of the Indian's protests, the white man continued his extermination for the robes which were in demand and for the tongues and humps which he used for food, thus leaving the prairies strewn with thousands of pounds of rotting meat, a disgraceful waste of a natural resource. The wolves, coyotes, and carrion birds never fared so well. No wonder the Indians soon began to do battle with the buffalo hunters. They realized that this cruel and useless slaughter would inevitably mean their own destruction.

The government encouraged this destruction as a means of subjugating the Indians by removing their chief source of food and clothing. President Grant had no sympathy for those who would stop the slaughter, and when a bill to regulate buffalo hunting was passed by Congress, he let it die for lack of his signature. General Phil Sheridan praised the hunters because they were destroying the commissaries of the Plains Indians and driving them onto reservations more effectively than the army.

This wholesale destruction helped open the American West. It aided in controlling the Indians, thus opening the range for cattle raising and bringing white adventurers into hitherto unexplored lands where many of them settled. Lastly, it helped some settlers make a livelihood by gathering the tons of bleached bones scattered over the prairies and shipping them to the manufacturers of fertilizer, bone china, buttons, and knife handles. This unique industry carried many early settlers through their first hard years; thus the destruction of the buffalo became a stage in the evolution of Western America. The hunters, Gard points out, were mighty men. He writes:

On the bleak Western plains they outlasted blizzards and sandstorms and, in most instances, outshot and outwitted the redskins who wanted their scalps. Usually the hunter was a young but grizzled and uncouth fellow, itchy from crawlers out of the piles of hides about his camp. Yet he knew how to dodge the charge of a wounded buffalo bull, and he used his heavy rifle with a precision that even a Prussian field marshal would have admired. At the bar of a frontier outpost, when his work was done, he could outdrink even the thirstiest cowpuncher (*The Great Buffalo Hunt*, p. v).

For the first time, this great slaughter is described in comprehensive detail, telling of the methods of the hunter's killing and of his battles for survival. As in most of his other books, Gard reserves a late chapter to devote to song and legend, by which he regales the reader with amazing tales of riding wild buffaloes and of finding refuge from blizzards by crawling into a warm buffalo carcass.

"Stories from the campfires of buffalo hunters on the windswept plains could have provided grist for many a Baron Munchausen," writes Gard. "Some of the tales were of unusual stands and big killings. Others were of narrow escapes from the charges of wounded bulls. More than a few told of finding cover in a blizzard that swept suddenly down on the open ranges. Most have been lost because neither the tellers nor the listeners bothered to put them in writing" (p. 276).

There were a few songs about the buffalo hunter, but Gard admits that "buffalo hunters were less inclined to song than were the Western cowboys, who sometimes sang to their charges on the long trail or crooned lullabies to the sleeping herd. It was hard to find anything romantic about shooting, skinning, and butchering the stinking animals. And in their camps at night, after a dinner of hump and tongue, the men were usually too tired to think of singing" (p. 289).

In this book's numerous annotations, one sees evidence of prodigious research. The author's meticulous regard for detail is evidenced throughout in citations from memoirs, diaries, reminiscences, and newspaper reports. Like Gard's other books, this one contains a full bibliography and useful index. It was published in the fall of 1959 by Alfred A. Knopf, who took enough personal interest in it to edit the manuscript himself.

Soon after its publication, *The Great Buffalo Hunt* became the choice of the Outdoor Life Book Club, which sold its members more than 35,000 copies. In addition, many copies were sold through bookstores. In 1968, with the cloth edition still in print, the University of Nebraska Press issued an attractive paperback edition with the same illustrations in its series of Bison Books.

Reviews were uniformly favorable and enthusiastic. Agnes Wright Spring wrote: "With sureness and in picturesque phraseology, the author portrays a grippingly accurate backdrop of one of the most dramatic periods in the history of the Western frontier. When you have finished the book, you will feel that you actually knew the Mooar brothers, Jim White, Marshall Sewell, and many, many more" (*Colorado Magazine*, XXXVII, April, 1960, 151-52).

In the *Mississippi Valley Historical Review*, David M. Vigness wrote in part:

> What is particularly striking to this reviewer is the meticulous regard for detail that the author maintains, evidencing prodigious research. Countless names are introduced, giving a sense of personality to a subject which otherwise might be handled in generalities only. . . . This detail is accomplished through heavy dependence upon memoirs, diaries, and reminiscences of participants of the chase. It might be added without detracting from the author's skill or credit, that the relative shortness of the entire episode of killing the buffalo contributed to the unity of the story. Mr. Gard, with his journalistic skill, has given us a book as gripping as a novel without destroying the impression of historical authenticity (XLVII, June, 1960).

Stanley Walker, in the *New York Herald Tribune*, wrote: "The author, Wayne Gard, a Dallas journalist and historian, is one of the most thorough and indefatigable researchers in the business, and his well documented account surely tells just about all that anyone needs to know about the passing of the buffalo. The literature on the subject is considerable, for many of the old buffalo killers left voluminous notes, and so did the bone-gathers who came after them. Mr. Gard makes a coherent picture of the whole grisly era" (October 25, 1959).

While on vacation in September of 1958, Gard was the dinner speaker on the subject of the buffalo hunter at the annual meeting of the Nebraska State Historical Society at Lincoln. In June of 1959 he interrupted his work to return to Illinois College, where he was awarded the honorary degree of Doctor of Literature.

In 1960 Gard began contributing an occasional book review to the New York Times Book Review. Over the years, several of his magazine articles were included in anthologies of various types, and he was invited to contribute chapters to others. Of these, the most important was a chapter entitled "The Law of the American West," which he wrote for The Book of the American West, published by Julian Messner late in 1963. This large and handsomely illustrated gift book, published in both a trade edition and a leather-bound deluxe volume in slip case, was later taken over by Simon and Schuster. There are ten chapters by ten different authors, each an expert on his subject, the whole dealing with practically every subject of the American West.

This extra writing was done in the hours left after his full-time newspaper work, mostly in the evenings and on holidays. He continued at the office to write editorials and articles assigned him on political, economic, and various other subjects, many of which brought responses from readers. For a number of years in the latter part of his work for the News, he edited the paper's letters from readers. Frequently he met with visitors of the editorial staff, often at private breakfast or luncheon, many of whom were such distinguished men as Henry Cabot Lodge and Lyndon B. Johnson.

At the beginning of 1964 Gard retired from the staff of the News at the age of sixty-four and a half, a year ahead of his mandatory date. During the few months following his retirement, he completed the revision and retyping of his seventh book, his sixth on Western history. This book, *Rawhide Texas*, is the only one he has written which is devoted entirely to Texas. It is a series of sketches on the various aspects of pioneer life in the state.

When there is no longer a grandpa around to tell what pioneer life was like in Texas "in the old days," much of this information can be found in this book of Gard's. It reveals the "long and often heroic conquest of the discouraging conditions that most settlers faced as the frontier was pushed westward." *Rawhide Texas* is packed with colorful anecdotes that throw light on how Texas and Texans came to be what they are. It tells of summer drouths, winter blizzards, and occasional tornadoes and hurricanes. It recounts raids by savage Comanches, attacks by predatory beasts, and fires that swept fields and pastures. It describes swarms of hungry grasshoppers that darkened the skies and devoured many crops. The pioneer, the author notes, "had to be as tough as the rawhide he braided into quirt and lariat. Only the sturdy survived."

The farmer and the herdsmen are only two of the many types of frontiersmen who appear in these pages. There was the saddle-bag preacher who swam his horse across swollen streams and traveled great distances to reach some settlement where he expected to preach for small compensation. "For this traveling, preaching, comforting the stricken, and burying the dead," writes the author, "even in the latter days of circuit riding, the preacher might receive one hundred to six hundred dollars a year, but he seldom collected all that was promised him" (*Rawhide Texas*, p. 128). There is the frontier doctor ready to ride fifty miles to set a broken bone or deliver a baby. Not only were doctors scarce on the frontier, but many of them were deficient in training as well. Yet they were willing to go difficult distances under all sorts of handicaps to do their best with their crude instruments and lack of proper remedies. And they did all this knowing that the fee, though small, would be difficult to collect.

The author tells of the schoolteachers who sometimes lost their lives from Indian massacres. If a man teacher, he also had to fight the larger boys to control them. "Country schools," writes Gard, "in which readin' and writin' and 'rithmetic were taught to the tune of a hickory stick were unusually hard to maintain on the Texas frontier. Settlers' homes were often far apart, qualified teachers hard to find, and textbooks scarce. The pupils had to trudge across the prairie or ride horseback, carrying their lunch pails" (p. 142).

This book also tells of the frontier editors who often had to carry a pistol to defend the freedom of the press. They were a fearless lot, unafraid to express their opinions in print. Yet they did not spend all their time exposing wrongdoing and quarreling with subscribers. They were also great boosters for the towns in which they took pride in trying to build up. "In the frontier period, as later," writes Gard, "the country editor was a constructive force and a community leader. Along with politicians, lawyers, and others, he served on civic and promotional committees. He was generous with his newspaper space not only to attracting settlers, railroads, and industries but in building roads, schools, and churches and upgrading cultural life. Without the economic rewards of the banker, the land speculator, or the ranchman, he worked as hard as any of them for the progress of his community" (p. 159).

Rawhide Texas tells of frontier amusements, such as horse racing and rooster fighting, of hunting bears and javelinas, of travel by stagecoach, of the trials in courts in which the judge's bench was a packing-box. It traces the building of railroads, the discovery of oil, and finally the blossoming of cultural interests in literature and the arts. From frontier years down through modern days, Texans have developed a taste for good literature, grand opera, and symphony music. "Since the days of their first dugouts, log cabins, and adobe huts," writes the author, "Texans have been a singing people. Perhaps only pioneers with a song in their hearts would have had the courage to tackle and tame the wilderness they faced. Even in combat, early Texans went forward singing and shouting" (p. 206).

Rawhide Texas was published by the University of Oklahoma Press in May of 1965. Like his other books, this one has a comprehensive bibliography and an index. Again the reviews were favorable. Tomme Call, reviewer for the *Corpus Christi Caller-Times*, wrote: "Forget the Westerns on television and the pulp magazine stories. This is the way it was, no paradise, no endless series of fabulous adventures, but a century of struggle to tame the wilderness. And it makes good reading" (June 13, 1965). Dean C. L. Sonnichsen wrote: "It is a rich and varied collection of every sort of information about the early Texans and how they lived. It could have been written only by a seasoned historian who has steeped himself for many years in the lore of the country, written and oral. The book reads easily, holds interest, and brings important segments of American history into perspective" (*New Mexico Historical Review*, XL, January, 1966, 71-73).

Gard's first chapter, "Eye on the Weather," tells of that tragic Galveston storm of 1900 and of the cyclone at Sherman during which many freakish things occurred, such as babies being blown from their mothers' arms and never found and photographs being driven into tree trunks without breaking. In the book, too, he recalls a few tall tales, mainly on the weather, but is careful not to vouch for them.

Less than a year after *Rawhide Texas* was published, Gard received the annual Summerfield G. Roberts award of $1000 sponsored by the Sons of the Republic of Texas. This award is given for the best book judged to portray "the spirit, character, strength, and deeds of men and women during the Republic of Texas days." The year before publication of this social history of the people of Texas (1964), Gard was invited to read a paper before the annual conference of the Western History Association in Oklahoma City, and he read from this manuscript the chapter on frontier editors.

He has edited and written an introduction for the manuscript of an earlier writer, *Up the Trail in '79* by Baylis John Fletcher. This little book was first published serially in the *Cattleman* and in 1966 was issued by the University of Oklahoma Press as Volume 37 in its *Western Frontier Library Series*. It contains a chapter devoted to the Big Spring robbery of the Union Pacific, in which there are several errors. Perhaps Gard felt that he had no right to correct another's manuscript, but as a historian with his knowledge of this event, it would have been well if he had called the the reader's attention to these errors through footnotes.

By invitation, he also wrote a chapter on the Chisholm Trail for *Along Early Trails of the Southwest* (Pemberton Press, Austin, Texas, 1969). His is one of the longer chapters of the book, and he deals with the Chisholm Trail in much the same way as he did in his own book of that title. Again he describes the route of the trail, the rustler and Indian troubles, the cowboy and his duties on the trail, the cook and his importance, and the rowdy cow town at the end of the trail.

Shortly after Gard's retirement, the editors of the *Encyclopedia Americana* asked him to contribute a number of short historical and biographical sketches on Western subjects for volumes then in the process of revision. By the middle of 1969 he had written twenty-four of these on such subjects as cattle branding, the Chisholm Trail, Sam Bass, Roy Bean, James Bowie, and David Crockett—all familiar subjects to him.

These articles were in line with what he had done earlier for the *Book of Knowledge* and the *Handbook of Texas*. He had contributed twenty-five such articles to the two-volume *Handbook*, published by the Texas State Historical Association in 1952; and he now has sixteen in a supplemental third volume.

Early in 1967 the trustees of his church, the First Unitarian, asked Gard to write as a contribution a booklet history of the church, which had been organized in 1899. He did a great deal of research on this subject and completed a 16,000-word manuscript in August, 1968. Publication of the booklet had been planned for the fall of that year, but stringency in church funds caused an indefinite postponement of the project.

During the years after his retirement, Gard had more time to write, yet he did not make a strenuous task of it.

During this time he devoted much time to the work of the Texas Chrisholm Trail Centennial Commission, to which Governor John Connally appointed him in 1966. More time was devoted to the Texas State Historical Association, of which, after progressing through four vice-presidencies, he was elected president in 1968.

In 1964 Gard was asked to write the Introduction to *If I Can Do It Horseback* by John Hendrix and published by the University of Texas Press. This is an interesting book by a talented writer who, when he lived, was a regular contributor to *Cattleman*. Hendrix was an experienced cowboy and ranchman who had an exceptional talent for describing the things and the life he wrote about.

In 1970 Gard contributed a pamphlet to Steck-Vaughn's Southwest Writers Series entitled *Reminiscences of Range Life*. In this pamphlet he writes of twenty-two different cattlemen—some ranchers, some cowboys, one sheepman, and even one woman. Though there are many books that Gard could have included in this work, he selected carefully to give the reader tabloid accounts of each character, telling of his experiences and accomplishments. Gard recognizes that those who have written reminiscences of range life were more adept with the rope than with the pen and that "choosing the twenty-two from a much larger number has not been easy. In general the books that seem more important or interesting are free from fictionizing and are more easily found" (*Reminiscences of Range Life*, p. iii).

Gard intentionally omitted discussion of the professional writers who knew range life at firsthand such as Charles A. Siringo, Andy Adams, Eugene Manlove Rhodes, and Ross Santee, each of whom has been treated in a separate pamphlet in the Southwest Writers Series.

Gard's *Reminiscences of Range Life* starts with *The Life of Tom Candy Ponting*, one of the first men to trail cattle from Texas to Northern markets. Other reminiscences discussed are Granville Stuart's *Forty Years on the Frontier*, John Clay's *My Life on the Range* (one of the better books), and William French's *Some Recollections of a Western Ranchman* (another wise choice).

Among other reputable cattlemen, Gard writes about James H. Cook, *Fifty Years on the Old Frontier*; Frank Hastings, *A Ranchman's Recollections*; Harry H. Halsell, *Cowboys and Cattleland: My Autobiography*; and John H. Culley, *Cattle, Horses and Men of the Western Range*.

Cowboys are not overlooked by Gard. Some about whom he writes are Edward Charles (Teddy Blue) Abbott, *We Pointed*

Them North; James Emmit McCauley, *A Stove-Up Cowboy's Story*; John Leakey, *The West That Was: From Texas to Montana*; Bob Kennon, *From the Pecos to the Powder: A Cowman's Autobiography*; Will S. James, *27 Years a Mavrick or Life on a Texas Range.*

Among the more recent books Gard writes about Ed Lemmon, *Boss Cowman: The Recollections of Ed Lemmon*; Jim Herron, *Fifty Years On the Owl Hoot Trail*; and Mat Ennis Jones, *Fiddlefooted.*

Gard did not overlook the ranchwoman. He included Mrs. Robert L. Duke of the famous XIT Ranch, *6000 Miles of Fence.* Neither did he overlook the sheepman for he included Archer B. Gilfillan, *Sheep Life on the South Dakota Range*, which is probably the best of all of the books on sheep and sheep herding.

Though Gard's *Reminiscences of Range Life* is in no way a digest or complete bibliography of all of the range reminiscences, it is, in Gard's usual accurate and clear style, an introduction to the literature of the range. He provides an excellent list at the end of this work for further reading, mentioning a few of the lesser rare books, but largely limiting the list to books that are available either in reprints or in larger libraries. This pamphlet is an excellent addition to the Southwest Writers Series.

Sometimes Gard is asked which of his six books on Western history is the best or his favorite. To this question he has replied:

> That is hard to answer. I have sentimental attachments to all of them, yet I realize the drawbacks of each. Obviously two are my favorites: *The Chisholm Trail* and *The Great Buffalo Hunt* are head and shoulders above the others in their contribution to historical knowledge. *The Great Buffalo Hunt* has an advantage in being more nearly a continuous narrative. *The Chisholm Trail* probably is a little better written. That is true partly because more material was available, thus allowing more choice, and partly because the nature of much of the material lent itself more to a semi-literary treatment. The cowboys, in spite of their isolation on the trail, weren't quite as far from civilization as were the buffalo hunters.

Judging from the bibliography of Gard's magazine writings, he appears to be rather prolific in this field. He started writing for magazines soon after his graduation from college in 1921. After his return to the United States from Burma and his return to full-time newspaper work in Des Moines in 1930, he wrote many articles on political and economic subjects, some of them the outgrowth of his newspaper editorial writings. For *Current History* he wrote half-a-dozen thoroughly researched articles on labor and farm problems, with such subjects as "The Injunction Process in Labor Disputes," "The Problem of Employment Agencies," "Agriculture's Industrial Revolution," "Decline in the Cotton Kingdom," "America's Desolate Acres," and "The American Peasant." For the *North American Review*, one of the country's oldest and most scholarly magazines, since discontinued, he treated topics like the St. Lawrence Seaway, the drive against noise, and the revival of river freight traffic. For *Vanity Fair*, also discontinued, he wrote lively articles on such subjects as the keg wine business, nepotism in Congress, mounting election costs, and the rising demand for military pensions. For *The Nation* he wrote on farm tariffs and the 1932 farm rebellion, on county consolidation for *Nation's Business*, and on adult education for the *Rotarian*. For both *The New Republic* and *American Mercury* he wrote on hot oil produced in excess of imposed quotas. For *House and Garden* he discussed the war on billboards. He wrote on marijuana, child labor, and the poll tax for *The Christian Century*, and articles on publicity trickery and funeral costs for *Plain Talk*.

Colorful personalities also were the subjects of some of his articles. He wrote of Ohio's General Coxey for *Vanity Fair* and on Oklahoma's Alfalfa Bill Murray and Texas's Pappy O'Daniel for *The New Republic*. So we see that in his earlier writings he dealt with many diversified and current subjects, as do most editorial writers.

But within three years after his move to Texas in August, 1933, he turned to Texas and Western historical subjects and began writing principally for a different group of regional and national magazines. Some of these articles stemmed from material he was gathering for his books on Western history.

Since then he has written on cattle rustling and buffalo hunting for *American Heritage* and on life in the Texas Republic for *American West*. His five articles in *Southwestern Historical Quarterly* have included cattle trails, buffalo hunters, and the Texas fence-cutting war of 1883.

His twenty-seven articles for the *Cattleman* have told of frontier horses and horse racing, cattle trailing, buffalo hunting, attempts at rainmaking, Teddy Roosevelt's wolf hunt, and such hazards as prairie fires, blizzards, and grasshopper plagues. For many years *Cattleman* issued an enlarged edition on horses each September, and Gard wrote horse articles for ten of them. He wrote about a Texas painter for *American Artist* and on Texas ranch houses for *Better Homes and Gardens*.

His eighteen articles for *Texas Parade* discussed, among other subjects, Texas weather, the Butterfield Trail, the slaughter of wild pigeons, the camel experiment, the fence-cutting war, troubles on the cattle trails, sheep, Indians on the warpath, prairie fires, buffaloes, and Texas folk songs. For the Texas edition of *Progressive Farmer* he wrote seventeen stories on such subjects as Western mirages, county-seat wars, frontier railroad building, the National Cowboy Hall of Fame, pioneer schools, drouths, horse racing, various Texas rivers, and cattle trails.

He has written ten articles for *Western Horseman* on such subjects as Bass's Denton Mare, lawmen on horseback, cowboy songs, horse thieves, the rodeo, horses on the cow trail, quarter horses, and horse racing; three articles for *Quarter Horse Journal* (the subjects of which were Steel Dust, Shiloh, and horse racing); one article on the cattle trails for *Humble Way*; one article entitled "The Role of the Cattle Trails" for *Nebraska History*; one article on javelinas for a Houston magazine no longer published; and one article entitled "The Myth of Deadwood Dick" for *Frontier Times*.

Concerning the character of Deadwood Dick, Gard writes:

In the case of most legendary figures, such as Robin Hood, it is impossible to learn much about the original person who gave rise to the stories or to trace precisely the steps by which reality became encrusted with fiction. In the instance of

Deadwood Dick, however, a curtain can be opened to reveal the origin of the myth and some—though not all—of the stages in its evolution.

While most folk heroes probably had their origins in real persons, Deadwood Dick sprang into life full-blown as a purely fictional character. Only later did flesh-and-blood men claim to have been the person on whose experiences the fictional tales were based (*Frontier Times*, XLIII 10).

Though this fictional character was created by the dime novelist Edward Lytton Wheeler of Philadelphia, there were at various times six different men, including one Negro, who claimed to be the original Deadwood Dick. As a historian, Gard never has hesitated to buck accepted concepts which the facts seemed to warrant. Several reference works had had items on Deadwood Dick as if he were a real person; but in 1968, when the *Encyclopedia Americana* asked Gard to write a short piece on this subject, he wrote one which showed that this character never existed except as a fictional character and that all these claimants were revealed as pretenders. His debunking of this character was expanded in more detail in a paper which he read at the annual meeting of the Texas Folklore Society in Dallas in 1969 and which, later that year, was published as an article in *Frontier Times* as mentioned above.

In 1953 Gard wrote an article for *Real Magazine* on the Boneheads Club of Dallas, a unique organization of that city. Other than his articles on buffalo hunting in *American Heritage*, perhaps his most reprinted article was one of the eight he wrote for *Southwest Review*, "Rooster Fight," appearing in 1935. This was a description of an all-day cocking main which he attended in a clubhouse in the woods near Corsicana, Texas. His other seven articles in *Southwest Review* were on such subjects as Sam Bass, quarter horses, frontier feuds, buffalo hunters, cattle and sheep wars, and food on the cattle trails. Two of his articles have appeared in *True West*, one of them a reprint in its entirety of his *Fabulous Quarter Horse: Steel Dust*.

From 1937 onward, nearly all of Gard's magazine articles have pertained to Texas and Western history, now his chief interest.

Some of them were the outgrowth of shorter articles in the *Dallas Morning News*; others embodied material he had gathered for use in one or another of his books. Others still were requested by editors of regional or national magazines. Even since his retirement he continues to write book reviews for the *News* and various learned magazines.

The style of writing in the books of Wayne Gard is so disarmingly simple that it might seem to some that there is no style at all. Yet that assumption would be a mistake. Gard writes mainly of people who live close to the soil, and he talks about them and their activities in grassroots language. Decades of writing for newspapers have taught him to avoid trite words and expressions and to use no more words than are necessary. Relatively short sentences and short paragraphs help make his writing easy to read.

He also has developed a skill in picking out the colorful and significant aspects of a person, a scene, or a situation. His writing is always clear and direct, never pompous or involved. Occasionally he uses figures of speech, but he does not overdo them or strain for forced effects. In addition, his transitions are so smooth that the narrative flows easily from one subject to the next.

His subjects are interesting, his books well organized, and his historical facts dependable. Compared with other Western historians, he may seem less romantic than some because he sticks to facts and does not invent unrecorded conversation for the sake of creating more interesting reading. To him, history comes first, and romance is left to the writers of romance. His works preserve the history of the great American West.

Selected Bibliography

BOOKS BY WAYNE GARD

Book Reviewing (New York: Alfred A. Knopf, 1927). Out-of-print.
Sam Bass (Boston: Houghton Mifflin Company, 1936). Out-of-print. Paperback edition (Lincoln: University of Nebraska Press, 1969).
Frontier Justice (Norman: University of Oklahoma Press, 1954).
The Chisholm Trail (Norman: University of Oklahoma Press, 1954).
Fabulous Quarter Horse: Steel Dust (New York: Duell, Sloan and Pearce, 1958). Out-of-print.
The Great Buffalo Hunt (New York: Alfred A. Knopf, 1959). Paperback edition (Lincoln: University of Nebraska Press, 1968).
Rawhide Texas (Norman: University of Oklahoma Press, 1965).

BOOK EDITED BY WAYNE GARD

Fletcher, John Baylis, *Up the Trail in '79* (Norman: University of Oklahoma Press, 1968).

PAMPHLETS BY WAYNE GARD

Cattle Brands of Texas (First National Bank in Dallas, 1956). Out-of-print.
The First 100 Years of Texas Oil and Gas (Dallas: Texas Mid-Continent Oil and Gas Association, 1966).
Reminiscences of Range Life (Austin: Steck-Vaughn Company, 1970).

MAGAZINE ARTICLES BY WAYNE GARD
(Partial list, including only articles on the West)

AMERICAN ARTIST
"Joe Ruiz Grandee, Painter of the Old West," XXXI (June, 1967), 56-63, 82-86.

AMERICAN HERITAGE
"Cattle Rustling and Rustlers' Wars," IV (Fall, 1952), 34-35, 64.
"How They Killed the Buffalo," VII (August, 1956), 34-39.

AMERICAN MERCURY
"Hot Oil from Texas," XXXV (May, 1935), 71-76.
"Texas Comes of Age" (under pen name), XXXVIII (June, 1936), 213-20.

40

"Sagebrush Justice," LXVI (April, 1948), 476-81.
"When Editors Were Men," LXVIII (January, 1949), 91-98.

AMERICAN WEST
"Life in the Land of Beginning Again," V (May, 1968), 42-49.

BETTER HOMES AND GARDENS
"The Ranchhouse Goes to Town," XV (June, 1937), 32-33, 52, 67.

CATTLEMAN
"Necktie Parties for Horse Thieves," XXXIV (September, 1947), 54, 57-58, 80.
"The Fence-Cutters," XXXIV (February, 1948), 38, 40, 43-44, 46, 48.
Reprinted from the Southwestern Historical Quarterly.
"Fabulous Steel Dust," XXXV (September, 1948), 50, 161-63, 165-67.
"Airborne Invader—the Grasshopper," XXXVI (July, 1949), 42, 44, 46, 48.
"Horsemen for the Lord," XXXVII (September, 1949), 44-45.
"Rustlers on the Open Range," XXXVI (March, 1950), 26, 109-10.
"When Fire Seared the Prairies," XXXVI (May, 1950), 35-37.
"Cow Horses on the XIT Ranch," XXXVII (September, 1950), 36, 68, 70, 146.
"Blizzards on the Range," XXXVII (January, 1951), 25, 61.
"In the Dallas Corral," XXXVII (March, 1951), 24-25, 52.
"Better Grass for More Beef," XXXVII (May, 1951), 24, 26, 28, 30, 32.
"Rainmakers Sell New Magic," XXXVIII (June, 1951), 76-78.
"Buckaroos for Fun," XXXVIII (September, 1951), 154-55.
"Midwest Cattle Kings," XXXVIII (October, 1951), 94, 96, 98.
"Before Barbed Wire," XXXVIII (January, 1952), 28.
"Roping Buffaloes on the Plains," XXXVIII (March, 1952), 35, 74, 76.
"Playing Politics with Braceros," XXXVIII (April, 1952), 96-98.
"Profit in Pint-Size Ponies," XXXIX (September, 1952), 62, 151-52.
"Still a Kick in Texas Mules," XXXIX (September, 1952), 80, 148, 150.
"Grub for the Trail," XXXIX (December, 1952), 60, 62, 64-65.
"Opening the Chisholm Trail," XXXIX (February, 1953), 146, 148-49.
"The Shawnee Trail," XXXIX (May, 1953), 30, 32, 34, 36, 38, 52, 54-59.
Reprinted from the Southwestern Historical Quarterly.
"Abilene in Its Glory," XL (June, 1953), 26, 60, 62.
"Hoofbeats of Old Shiloh," XL (September, 1953), 39, 66, 70, 72.
"Texas' Fence-Cutting War," XL (November, 1953), 24, 86, 88, 90. Reprinted from Texas Parade.
"Salt on the Range," XL (December, 1953), 28, 42.
"New Agreement on Braceros," XL (April, 1954), 52-55.
"The Denton Mare," XLI (September, 1954), 50, 112.
"Horsehead Crossing," XLI (December, 1954), 21, 34, 36.
"Indian Horses," XLII (September, 1955), 41, 72, 74, 76.
"Hunting Buffaloes in Texas," XLII (November, 1955), 42, 65-66, 68.
"Butterfield Trail Centennial," XLII (February, 1956), 33, 54, 56.

"On a Ten-Dollar Horse," XLIII (September, 1956), 52, 54, 56, 58.
"Hunting Bears in Texas," XLIV (February, 1958), 31, 40, 42.
"Teddy Roosevelt's Wolf Hunt," XLIV (October, 1958), 25, 38, 40, 42.
Reprinted in *True West*, August, 1962.
"Buffalo Hunters at Work," XLV (February, 1959), 33, 62, 64, 66-68.
"Gathering Buffalo Bones," XLV (March, 1959), 53-54, 56, 58, 60, 62, 67.
"Chisholm Trail Centennial," LII (October, 1965), 67-68.

HUMBLE WAY
"Up the Chisholm Trail," VI (Second Quarter, 1967), 11-15.

NEBRASKA HISTORY
"The Role of the Cattle Trails," XXXIX (December, 1958), 287-301.

THE NEW REPUBLIC
"Alfalfa Bill," LXX (February 17, 1932), 11-12.
"Hot Oil," LXXXI (January 30, 1935), 326-27.
"Texas Kingfish," CIV (June 23, 1941), 848-50.
"Bringing O'Daniel to Judgment," CVII (July 13, 1942), 49-51.

PROGRESSIVE FARMER (Texas edition)
"When Drouth Hit the Frontier," LXVII (August, 1952), 18, 90.
"Horse Racing on the Frontier," LXVIII (January, 1953), 17, 80.
"Where Buffalo Roamed," LXVIII (August, 1953), 18.
"Blackmail on the Chisholm Trail," LXIX (April, 1954), 23, 159.
"Comanche Moon," LXX (September, 1955), 27, 147.
"Pranks of the Mirage," LXXI (August, 1956), 90.
"The Brazos," LXXI (October, 1956), 29.
"The Red," LXXI (December, 1956), 25.
"The Colorado," LXXII (February, 1957), 29.
"Texas Had County-Seat Wars," LXXII (April, 1957), 42.
"The Pecos," LXXII (September, 1957), 34.
"Texas Railroad Fever," LXXII (December, 1957), 36.
"Texans Ride to Cowboy Fame," LXXV (May, 1960), 21. Reprinted in the Congressional Record.
"Restoring Order in Frontier Texas," LXXV (June, 1960), 34.
"When Texas Agriculture Spread Out," LXXVI (February, 1961), 36.
"The Civil War in the Southwest," LXXVI (May, 1961), 95.
"If You Think School Is Rough!" LXXIX (September, 1964), 66-67.

QUARTER HORSE JOURNAL
"Hoofbeats of Old Steel Dust," VII (December, 1954).
"On the Prairie Turf," VII (April, 1955).
"New Light on Old Shiloh," VIII (December, 1955).

REAL
"The Zany Boneheads of Dallas," II (August, 1953), 30-33, 84.

SOUTHWEST REVIEW
"Texas Robin Hood," XXI (October, 1935), 15-23.

"Rooster Fight," XXII (October, 1936), 65-70.
"The Quarter Horse," XXV (July, 1940), 419-28.
"Where the Mountains Meet," XXVI (Winter, 1941), 203-10.
"Frontier Vendetta," XXXIII (Spring, 1948), 146-53.
"Rivals for Grass," XXXIII (Summer, 1948), 266-73.
"Grub for the Trail," XXXVII (Summer, 1952), vii-xi, 253-54.
"Tales of the Buffalo Hunters," XLIV (Spring, 1959), 156-62.

SOUTHWESTERN HISTORICAL QUARTERLY
"The Fence-Cutters," LI (July, 1947), 1-15. Reprinted in Cattleman, February, 1948.
"The Shawnee Trail," LVI (January, 1953), 359-77. Reprinted in Cattleman, May, 1953.
"Retracing the Chisholm Trail," LX (July, 1956), 53-68.
"The Mooar Brothers, Buffalo Hunters," LXIII (July, 1959), 31-45.
"The Impact of the Cattle Trails," LXXI (July, 1967), 1-6.

TEXAS PARADE
"Reviving Old Preston Road," XII (November, 1951), 18-19.
"Of Texas We Sing," XII (February, 1952), 8-10.
"The Legend of Sam Bass," XIII (February, 1953), 29-31.
"Texas' Fence-Cutting War," XIV (July, 1953), 39-42. Reprinted in Cattleman, November, 1953.
"Wild Camels in Texas," XIV (August, 1953), 26-28. Reprinted in Line, July, 1954.
"Troubles on the Old Chisholm Trail," XIV (February, 1954), 19-21.
"New Crops for Texas," XIV (May, 1954), 47-49.
"On the Buffalo Range," XV (November, 1954), 41-43.
"On the Butterfield Trail," XV (February, 1955), 34-36.
"Plantation Days," XV (April, 1955), 33-36.
"Wool on the Hoof," XV (May, 1955), 29-32.
"Injuns on the Warpath," XVI (February, 1956), 29-31.
"Whirlybirds from Texas," XVI (March, 1956), 9-10.
"Texas Weather," XVII (November, 1956), 20-22.
"When Prairie and Forest Blaze," XVII (February, 1957), 36-37.
"When Wild Pigeons Darkened Texas Skies," XVII (March, 1957), 45, 47-49.
"Prickly Pear to the Rescue," XVII (April, 1957), 34-35.
"Along the Chisholm Trail," XXVIII (July, 1967), 20-21, 24.

TEXAS PREVIEW
"How To Hunt Javelinas," IV (January, 1953), 18-19, 25.

THINK
"Reclaiming Lost Lands of Texas," XX (February, 1954), 14-15, 33. Condensed in the Science Digest, July, 1954.

TRUE WEST

"Teddy Roosevelt's Wolf Hunt," IX (July-August, 1962), 34-35, 52. Reprinted from the *Cattleman*.

"Fabulous Quarter Horse: Steel Dust," XVI (July-August, 1969), 6-13, 44-52.

THE WEST

"Night Justice on Clear Fork," XII (March, 1970), 18-19, 44-46.

WESTERN HORSEMAN

"Sam Bass and His Denton Mare," XIII (July-August, 1948), 22-23, 56-59.

"Horsemen for the Law," XIII (November-December, 1948), 10-11, 37-38; and XIV (January, 1949), 13, 28, 30, 32.

"All the King's Horses," XIV (March, 1949), 14-15, 38-42.

"Singing on Horseback," XIV (May, 1949), 14-15, 38-41.

"When Texans Shouted for Shiloh," XIV (August, 1949), 14-15.

"Billy Anson, Quarter Horse Champion," XV (July, 1950), 17, 39-41.

"Frontier Hemp for Horse Thieves," XV (December, 1950), 11, 36-38.

"Grass-Roots Rodeo," XVII (July, 1952), 16-17, 40-41.

"Horses for the Cow Trail," XIX (April, 1954), 8-9, 30-31.

"Steel Dust in the Quarter Tracks," XIX (June, 1954), 19, 40-43.